Everybody's Chance

(John Habberton)

I -- HOW THEY HEARD OF IT

BRUNDY was the deadest town in the United States; so all the residents of Brundy said. It had not even a railway station, although several other villages in the county had two each. It was natural, therefore, that manufacturers' capital avoided Brundy. There was a large woolen mill at Yarn City, eight miles to the westward, and Yarn City was growing so fast that some of the farmers on the outskirts of the town were selling off their estates in building lots at prices which justified the sellers in going to the city to end their days. At Magic Falls, five miles to the northward, there was water power and a hardwood forest, which between them made business for several manufacturers of wooden-ware, as well as markets, with good prices for all farmers of the vicinity.

But Brundy had only land and people. The latter, according to themselves, were as good as the people anywhere, but the soil was so poor that no one could get a living out of it without very hard work. There was no chance of any kind for any of the natives. Young men were afraid to marry, and young women were afraid to marry them; for what girl wanted to go through the routine of drudgery in which she had pitied her own mother, and what lover wanted to ask his sweetheart to descend from the position of assistant at her old home to slave of all work in a new one?

The lack of a chance for any one had made itself manifest at Brundy many years before the date at which this story opens, so many of the natives had gone elsewhere to better their condition. The great majority of them had not been heard from afterward, so Brundy did not doubt that they had become too prosperous to think of their simple old friends and neighbors. Some, however, who had gone to great cities and the great West, had returned to the place of their birth to end their days, and they were so reserved as to how they had made their money, and how much they had made, that Brundy agreed that there were some great secrets of wealth to be discovered in the outside world, could the inhabitants of Brundy ever get away and search for it.

For instance, there was old Pruffett; he had gone to Chicago when barely twenty-one, remained there forty years, and been so busy all the while that he declared that he never had found time to look about him for a wife. He had made money, too; no one knew how much, and Pruffett never would tell, but as he paid cash for whatever he bought in the village and never haggled about prices, it seemed evident that he was very well off, for Squire Thomas, the richest native who had always remained at home, would never buy even a pound of butter until a penny or two of the price had been abated.

Sad though it be to relate, there were pretty and good young women in Brundy who would gladly have married old Pruffett for his money, and loving mothers who would have advised and helped them in that direction had old Pruffett given them any encouragement, but what could any one do with a millionaire-- so they called him-- who was satisfied to do his own work and do his own cooking in the cottage in which he was born, and which he had kept for years just as his mother left it when she died, and he had been too busy to hurry home to receive her dying blessing?

There was nothing mean about Pruffett; he contributed liberally to all church subscriptions, and when any neighbor chanced to fall into any trouble the old man was the first to offer counsel and substantial aid; still, why did he not be wholesouled and tell younger men how and where to find their chance in life-- the chance which Brundy persistently denied every one?

One morning the entire village was thrown into a fever of excitement and sarcasm by the appearance of the following notice, which was posted on the bulletin-board in front of the town hall and on trees in the several streets:

"Everybody has a Chance

"A lecture on the above subject will be given at the town hall next Friday night. The lecturer has nothing to sell, nor any medicines or other goods to recommend, nor anything to advertise. It is to be a square talk by a square man, who can prove what he says. No charge for admission; people who like the lecture may, if they desire, drop some small change into a box which will be at the door."

"Everybody has a chance, eh?" said the natives to one another. "That man doesn't know what sort of town he's coming to. If he is depending upon the collection at the door to help him to the next town he'll have to walk."

The more the lecturer's subject was discussed the more ridiculous it appeared, and as most people rather enjoy the spectacle of a man making a fool of himself the town hall was absolutely jammed on Friday night, half an hour before the usual time for the appearance on the platform of such strolling entertainers as did not know of the impecuniosity of the natives.

When the town clock struck eight the audience saw coming from the ante-room to the platform a middle-aged man with the garb and the eye of a well-to-do mechanic and the manner of a preacher, although he soon manifested an unpreacher-like disregard for grammatical rules. The lecture, too, although humorous enough at times to set every one laughing, was somewhat like a sermon in its general character.

"People talk about not havin' a chance," began the lecturer. "Why, if chances were eggs, none of you could move without steppin' on 'em. When a man says he hasn't got his chance in life he's talking about the particular chance he wants-- that's all. What we want most isn't always what we need most, my friends, though few of us are honest enough and smart enough to see it an' say so.

"I'd bet a dollar to a doughnut that the chance an' the only one-- that every man in this room is simply achin' for, so that he won't look at any other, is the chance to make a lot of money! Did he ever see anybody that had made a lot of money? Did the rich man look any happier than other folks? If not, why not? Can any of you tell the difference between the rich and the poor by their faces? I can't, except that generally the richest man looks most anxious and most discontented."

By this time every one in the house was looking at old Pruffett, who was looking at the back of the seat in front of him, although the expression of his countenance did not imply that there was anything particularly cheerful and inspiring in the back of that seat. The lecturer continued:

"An old book which all of you have in the house, and which some of you profess to believe with all your might, says that 'A man's life consisteth not in the abundance of the things which he possesseth'; you can read the passage for yourselves, and correct me if I am wrong. That same old book tells of chances that came to lots of people that hadn't a cent, either before or after. There are just as good chances now, and Brundy's as full of 'em as any other place, an' the people that don't get 'em are the people who won't see 'em, though if the chances were bears they'd bite 'em, they're so close. A man's best chance is whatever is closest to him; if it isn't also closest to his heart, that's the man's fault-- not the chance's."

The lecturer went on in the same vein, and told of some of his own chances which he had missed, as well as of some in which he had, to use his own expression, "caught on"; and he told some stories of personal experience so well that he made a lot of people cry a little, and laugh much, and not a few were compelled to do some serious thinking

When the talk ended there was quite a melodious jingling of coin in the box at the door; and several members of the audience who were nearest to old Pruffett told their neighbors for a week afterward that the old man actually dropped into the box a ten-dollar bill, forty times as much as would have paid the lecturer's stage fare to the next town.

"Got any small change about your clothes, Champ?" asked Charley Wurring, a smiling youth, of Champney Bruff, a serious-looking man of about thirty years, who was exploring his vest pocket. Charley had abundant reason for smiling, for by his side, where she had been throughout the lecture, was Luce Grew, the handsomest girl in the village. "I didn't bring any money, for I came only to laugh, but I found my chance during the lecture, and here she is, eh, Luce?"

Luce looked rather bashfully toward Champ with her great dark eyes and strong face, and then, for relief, smiled pleasantly at Charley. Champ flushed a little under his dark brown skin, but mechanically extended a coin toward Charley, who took it and dropped it into the box. Then he took Luce's hand, placed it on his arm, whispered something to the girl, which elicited a smile which Champ regarded fixedly, although the longer he looked the whiter and more fixed it became. Suddenly it appeared to him that old Pruffett was regarding him intently, and as he did not care to be looked at closely at that particular moment he abruptly left the hall and started homeward.

So Charley Wurring and Luce Grew had come to an understanding.

And Luce Grew was the one woman of Brundy whom Champney Bruff had ever thought he could love. Could love? Had he not loved her for years? He had not dared tell her so, for how could he? He was the oldest member of his father's family; his mother was dead, his father unfit for work; and the farm was one which required steady work and rigid economy if it was to support all of Champ's brothers and sisters. The farm would be better if he could clear and drain about twelve acres of marshy woodland that belonged to it, and to clear that land had been his special effort for two or three years; but after the usual farm routine had been gone through with, even in winter, he could find time to chop down only two or three trees a day, and after all the trees were gone there would still be the stumps, and after the stumps the ditching. When all this had been done, he would propose to Luce Grew, but now, evidently, his chance or his duty, which to the lecturer had seemed to mean the same thing, was the finishing of that clearing-- while Luce Grew loved another man and would marry him.

He heard footsteps behind him, and in a moment old Pruffett joined him with:

"Not a bad lecture, Champ?"

"Not for those who found their chances while the lecture was going on," was the reply, in words that sounded as if each had been savagely bitten off. There was a moment of silence before the old man said:

"I guess I know what you mean. I'm very sorry, too-- for you. Yet Luce herself seemed to be happy; I suppose that's what you've longed to see her? You'd have done anything to make her happy eh?"

"Yes; anything in my power."

"Good. Now's your chance."

"What on earth do you mean, Mr. Pruffett?"

"Merely what I say. If you loved her, not yourself, or loved her more than you loved yourself, you can do a great deal to make her happy; far more than Charley Wurring can."

"I wish I knew what you were trying to say, Mr. Pruffett."

"Do you? Then I'll try to make myself understood. Charley is a well-meaning fellow, but nowhere near enough of a man to marry a girl like that. Splendid girls sometimes accept a husband of that kind after waiting a long time in vain for a better one; the range of choice in this town is rather small, you know. Charley's much the best of his family; indeed, he hasn't any bad habits of his own, and he has learned to hate all that he might have inherited, but you know his fix; a father who has drunk himself into incapacity for anything, and a mother who is utterly discouraged and bad-tempered. Luce will have many occasions for feeling sorry for her choice; and Charley will often have to feel desperate, for what chance can he see, at present, of marrying and supporting a wife?"

"Well!" exclaimed Champ, savagely.

"Well, you know what the lecturer said about chances? Yours is right at hand-- right now. Why don't you put Charley into that wooded marshland of yours, to clear it? Give him the wood in payment; you'd not lose a cent by that. Get his father to help him, the weakest man has enough romance in him to want to help his son to a good wife. Work is the best cure for drunkenness, and the fellow daren't and can't drink while his son is with him all the while. By doing this you would be improving a chance to greatly benefit three people; such a chance seldom comes to any one."

"And I would also help another man to marry the woman whom--"

"Whom you love? Well, for what do you love her? For her sake or for your own?"

Champ remained silent; the old man went on:

"You don't seem to know. It's well, then, that you didn't chance to marry her."

"Mr. Pruffett," exclaimed Champ-- he almost roared it-- "do you know what you are saying? Are you human? Are you a man, like other men?"

"I am, my boy," replied the old man calmly. "I don't mind telling you, in strict confidence, that I loved Luce's mother-- God bless her!-- forty years ago. I never loved any other woman-- I tried to, but I couldn't. I had an awful fight with myself, after Grew won her, and I got the worst of it, for I was obliged, as an honest man, to admit to myself that I loved myself more than I loved her. To reform myself, I determined to go on loving her, but for her sake only, and the way I did it was to do just as I am advising you. I hadn't any marshland to clear, and there was nothing in Grew's family history for the young man to be ashamed of, but I put him into the one good chance which I had here, and I went away to shift for myself. I don't deny that I hoped that something would happen to break their engagement, but there didn't. I wish Luce were my daughter, for there's no one I would rather see her marry than you, but there are some things which one can't change-- some chances which a man loses. Your chance is just as I'm putting it; I'm advising only what I did myself, and what I never had cause to regret. I know, though, it isn't the sort of thing to press on a young man too hard, and I'm sure that, while you're in your present frame of mind, you don't care to listen to any more of this kind of talk, so-- good-night."

"Good-night," was the response, as sharp as the crack of a rifle.

"Shake hands with me, won't you, Champ?" said the old man softly. "No one else knows so well how to sympathize with you. Don't forget that I loved her mother-- and lost her."

They shook hands as they parted, but Champ's head was in a whirl, and his heart was thumping angrily. What? Help the man who had just taken from him the prize toward which he had been struggling for years? Pruffett had probably told the truth, but-- well, men were not all of the same clay. Love Luce for her own sake? Why, what else had he thought of but what he would do to make Luce happy? Had not his delay been entirely because of his doubts and fears for her? What was most in his mind whenever he thought of her-- himself? Never! He thought only of her-- her great, deep eyes, her noble face, her womanly composure, her strength of character everything that was best in womanhood, so far as he knew women. He was sure that through his very admiration of all that was best in her, he knew best how to make her happy, while Charley, a mere good-natured, happy-go-lucky fellow, who had seemed to be in love with half-a-dozen other girls for no especial reason, would be utterly unable to comprehend the needs of so superior a nature.

Yet there was some truth in what old Pruffett had said about the ways in which Charley could be helped to become a more fit husband. If some one else could help him, well and good, but as to Champ-- . He struggled hard with himself a few moments; then he suddenly stopped, bared his head, looked upward, and exclaimed:

"Heaven help me, I'll do it-- for her sake! 'Tis my chance-- but what a chance."

II -- IN THE CAMP OF THE ENEMY

Luce Grew told herself, after Charley had reluctantly gone home and she found herself alone with her thoughts, that she wondered how she had come to say "Yes" to the very pointed question which Charley Wurring had put to her during a certain point of the lecture. Charley had one of the sympathetic natures which are rare among men, or, perhaps, less rare than the willingness of their owners to manifest them, so Luce had always liked him. He was quick to see the application of an argument, or the inner and better sense of almost anything that might be said, so Luce had never failed to find him good company, although she regarded him very much as if he were a boy, although he was fully as old as she. She had been deeply interested in the lecture, and her better self approved all that the speaker said; so it pleased her greatly that when she looked at Charley for sympathy his face was frank and open, and he seemed to be of exactly her own way of thinking; while most of the young men about him were looking grim, or were sneering, or exchanging satirical winks with other young men.

So, when the lecturer told the hearers that their chances were all about them-- nay, right at their side, waiting only to be accepted, Charley had whispered:

"Luce, don't you think you could make a personal application of that remark? I am right at your side; won't you accept me? I won't ask any other or grander chance than you while I live."

She felt like laughing at the boy, but he looked so earnest, so manly, yet at the same time so appealing, that she did what many another woman has done in similar circumstances she began to wonder. Life was long; Brundy was a small place; there were other young men in the village, but very, very few whom she could by any possibility marry. She did not like the possibility of remaining single all her life. Charley was not the kind of man upon whom she had set her fancy, but young men were disappointing creatures; she had never been in love with one, but girls of her acquaintance had made dreadful mistakes in marrying men whom Luce herself had thought quite good. Charley was good-- she never had heard a word against him: he was very attentive to his mother and kind to his sisters. He had nothing upon which to marry, but engagements generally were long in Brundy; perhaps if she were to accept him it might be the means of making him everything he now failed to be.

"Does it take you so long to make up your mind?" whispered Charley. "I know I'm not worthy of you, but, on the other hand, neither is any one else; I'll be anything you wish, if you'll think me good enough to begin with."

She looked down into his eyes; they were very honest eyes, and at that particular instant they were very earnest. Luce blushed slightly and dropped her own eyes, Charley's hand sought hers, pressed it, and received a gentle pressure in return; then he whispered:

"Thank you. God bless you."

On the way home she talked to him kindly, but not enthusiastically; she told him that his proposal had been a great surprise, and perhaps she had accepted it too hastily, for she really had never thought of loving him; but Charley was so grateful, and so willing to wait, and so astonished at his own temerity, and so overwhelmed by his new joy, that she could not help being deeply affected, so she made but a single condition; the affair must be a secret between them until both of them were certain that they were not mistaken. Charley promised willingly, for he was concerned, for Luce's sake, about what people would say should they know of what had occurred. Marriage was a serious matter in Brundy, from the dollar and cents point of view; and he knew that every one in the village knew that he had neither money nor prospects, and that his only employment, thus far, had been several months of school teaching, during the winter months, and such occasional work as he could find in the village and among the farmers during the summer. He well knew, too, what people would say about a woman like Luce entering a family such as the Wurring family had become, through the habits of the head of the house.

The next morning, therefore, Charley made haste to find Champ, the only man to whom he had betrayed his feelings, and beg that young man to keep the matter a profound secret.

He found Champ in the marshland forest, working as if he were determined to fell all the trees in a single day. Champ rested upon his axe and kept his eyes on the ground while the communication was made; then, without raising his eyes, he said:

"What have you to marry on?"

"Not a cent," was the reply, "though here's the half dollar you lent me last night."

"Keep that to start your fortune with," said Champ. "There's money here for you if you choose to work for it."

"Here? Where? How?"

"By cutting away these trees. If you'll do it, and keep at the job until it is done, you may have all of the wood. Good firewood brings three dollars a cord in town during the winter months, which aren't far off, and the supply is none too great. There's at least a couple of hundred dollars' worth here, and I want it out of the way, but I've not the time to do it myself."

"'Tis mine, then!" exclaimed Charley joyously. "I'll go home at once for my axe."

"You needn't take that trouble," said Champ, anxious to get away from the spectacle of a man so happy, and from such a cause. "You may use mine for the remainder of the day. When you come back after dinner, perhaps you can persuade your father to help you; I'm sure he would do it if he knew the reason. Two pairs of hands are better than one at such a job, for 'twill be no easy one, I assure you."

"Thank you," said Charley. "I'll be glad to have my father with me, for reasons which I needn't explain to you. But, Champ, I feel as if I could do the whole job myself, in a very short time. Oh, I feel like a giant."

"Indeed?" was the reply, given almost with a sneer.

"Yes, indeed. Oh, you may look that way if you like, but you don't understand the feeling. Just wait, though, until you are fairly in love yourself, an'--"

"Oh, don't talk to me in that way," exclaimed Champ, biting his lips and turning aside; he felt that if he did not quickly get away he would fly at the fellow and strangle him.

"But I must talk so," persisted Charley, "and you are the only man to whom I can do it, for no one else knows of my great fortune but you. To think that I am the only man in the village who is so richly blessed. There's no other girl in Brundy who can compare with Luce; honestly now, old fellow, is there?"

Champ took his knife from his pocket and began to shave the rough bark from the coat of a slippery-elm tree.

"I do believe you think there is," said Charley, looking curiously at his companion, "and that you're in love with her. Oh, you sly chap! You always were the quietest young man in the town, and have seldom paid attention to any of the girls, but I do believe I have found you out. Who is she? I won't tell anybody. I'd like to know that some other man is as happy as I. Has she said 'Yes'?"

"Will you kindly attend to your own business and leave mine to me?" asked Champ, suddenly turning on Charley a face like a thunder-cloud. The younger man exclaimed quickly:

"I beg a thousand pardons, Champ. I didn't mean to be impertinent. You never saw anything like that in me, did you?"

"Not until a few moments ago," was the reply. "But I don't want ever to see it again."

"You shan't, I assure you," said Charley in haste, as he began to tone down his excitement by attacking the largest tree near at hand. He worked vigorously several moments, but finally stopped to say:

"Let me talk of Luce, though. She is so grand, so good, so unlike all other girls. I've thought myself in love before, but I soon found out 'twas all fancy." Charley leaned on his axe and looked contemplatively at the ground a moment or two before he continued: "Other girls seemed to like me to make love to them, but it soon became an old story to both of us, for they seemed to have nothing in their minds but what was trifling and merely romantic, but Luce-- why, there's something in the very tone of her voice that makes her seem different from every other young woman, and better. She's-- she's-- oh, she's thoroughly womanly, while the others are merely girlish. Don't you think that is the proper distinction, so far as you have observed her and other Brundy girls?"

As Charley asked this question he raised his eyes for the answer, but Champ was no longer standing before him. Charley looked slowly about him, but could see Champ nowhere; then he quickly peered between the trees, in every direction, and finally saw Champ, some distance away, walking rapidly and with his fingers to his ears.

"I declare," exclaimed the young man to himself, yet softly, as if he feared that even the trees had ears, "I believe I've been making a fool of myself. I didn't suppose, though, that a man generally so kind and sympathetic as Champ could have been quite so rude. Did I really say anything that was dreadfully silly?"

He thought a little while about it, and this naturally set him to thinking about Luce, and the subject was so interesting that he could not give any attention to anything else, so he leaned against a tree and indulged in delightful day-dreaming for he knew not how long. Neither could he afterward imagine how long he might have continued at his congenial occupation had he not been startled by a footfall, and, looking about him, seen Champ returning with an axe in his hand. Champ at first looked sheepishly toward him and said:

"I thought I could spare half a day to help you." When, however, the big fellow cast his eyes about and saw not a tree had been felled since he made his escape he glared savagely at Charley, and exclaimed:

"You're a fine fellow to think of marrying, aren't you? You've not chopped a stroke since I left you. I had better have offered this wood to a better man, even if I had been obliged to look for one not in love. I suppose you would like me to do all the work for you, after giving you the trees-- eh?"

Charley's face turned scarlet; he seized his axe and began to make chips fly rapidly. Champ also attacked a tree, and for a few moments no sound was heard but that of the axes upon the tree-trunks. Soon Charley wanted to stop, for he was unaccustomed to the work, and his hands had begun to blister, but after what Champ had said the young man was resolved to suffer anything rather than remain under the cruel imputation of being willing that Champ should earn the money on which the younger man should wed Luce Grew. Suddenly, however, to his great relief, Champ's tree fell, and the axeman stood aside for a moment.

"I covet your strength," exclaimed Charley; "and I'm going to have it, or something like it, if hard work will get it for me. A man who is to marry Luce Grew should have as much muscle as heart."

"Talk is cheap," responded Champ. After this there was nothing for Charley to do but attack his tree again. Soon, however, the blisters in his right hand began to break, and the pain was very like torture, so he laid down his axe and began to blow upon the palms of his hands. Champ approached him, took his hand roughly and looked at it. Then he looked inquiringly into Charley's face, and said:

"You're more of a man than I thought you. You can't go on with such a hand. Wait a moment."

He went to a hollow tree, and drew from it a pair of old leather gloves and a small bottle of oil.

"Here; put some of this on your hands, and put these gloves on. Once in a while I'm afflicted in the same way, after I've been out of axe practice a little while. Give the oil a few minutes in which to get in its work."

Champ returned to his tree, lopping off the boughs as if they were twigs, cutting them into four-foot lengths and tossing them aside; then he cut the trunk itself into four-foot lengths. Charley looked on in admiration, but while the giant looked about for another foeman worthy of his steel the younger man exclaimed:

"What a magnificent specimen of manhood you are! It is a man like you whom Luce should marry. I suppose, however, she knows her own mind."

"Whether she does-- or no--" said Champ, speaking between the strokes of his axe, "her mind is-- the only one she can go by-- for the present." Then he stopped a moment and said, "Can't you possibly talk of something else? You ought to be thinking and talking about how much you will do in a day, and asking who is most likely to buy the wood and pay quickest, and where you can best put your money at interest as fast as you collect it. Talking about a girl never helped a man to marry her; 'tis work-- nothing else-- that makes a man worthy of the love he pretends to bear a woman."

"I guess you're right, Champ," sighed Charley, addressing himself once more to work, "but I wish I knew where you got so much sense. I won't ask you any more about it, as it seemed to worry you a few minutes ago, but whoever the girl is that you're fond of, why, she's going to be the happiest woman alive."

"Umph, I hope so, but-- I shan't believe it-- until I-- see it."

"Come, now, old fellow, you shouldn't distrust yourself in that stupid manner. 'Faint heart never won fair lady'-- keep that saying close in mind. Why, it was the most daring thing in the world-- my proposing to Luce; I had everything against me, and I knew it; I took my chances, though, and you know what came to pass. If you would only see yourself as you are, and as everybody else sees you, and as the girl herself can't help seeing, and--"

"Will you be quiet?" exclaimed Champ, suddenly turning with a threatening face and with his axe still uplifted.

"No, I won't," replied the younger man, with a calm but determined face. "You've done me a great favor this morning, and I want to do you one in return. You may think that I want to pry into your affairs, but I don't. I want to tell you, though, what the lecturer told all of us last night, that every man has his chance in life, that it is very close to him, and that only he is to blame if he won't see it. To be happily in love is the one thing you need to make you as happy as you are manly, and I'm sure that's saying a great deal. Instead of that you're belittling yourself. You're my friend; you've done more for me this morning than any other man ever did, and until I can do something equally good for you I want to ease my mind by giving you some good advice. You ought to do just what I have done, determining, as I did, that whatever else had to be done afterward I would do with all my might, or make a better man of myself while failing. Why don't you do it? Have you proposed yet?"

"No!"

"Doesn't the girl even know that you love her?"

"No. I don't see, at least, how she can know it."

"That's bad-- for her. 'Twould make life a very different thing for any woman in this dead-and-alive town to know that a man like you cared for her. Women in Brundy-- young women-- have a pretty dismal outlook. I'm not going again to ask you who she is, but I do wish I knew, for I'd take the responsibility of telling her; after that she'd wait forever, and be happy in spite of anything, to know that there was such great good fortune in store for her."

"You'd tell her, would you?" snarled Chump. "I've a great mind to let you, just to see what a flunk you would make of it, you--"

"I dare you to do it," said Charley, meeting Champ's scowl without flinching. The older man glared furiously, and suddenly betook himself again to his axe, dashing at the tree as if it were his rival himself. But Charley's blood also was up, and he went on, shouting so that his words should not be drowned by the shower of axe-strokes.

"Yes, I dare you. I don't care a bit for your temper; you're a first-rate fellow in spite of it, and the woman who doesn't know that you love her shall know it at once if I can find out who she is."

Champ faced about, dropped his axe, controlled his face, and said, with manly dignity:

"She is Luce Grew."

"Luce!" exclaimed Charley, staggering backward.

"Yes, Luce. Now do you know why you won't tell her? It is because I love her, and want her to be happy, that I've thrown this job into your hands this morning. She has accepted you; well, that is her own business, and her own right, and no one else has the slightest use for complaining. But mark my words, young man. I never shall annoy her in any way, but I shall never cease to love her. On the other hand, if you fail to be to her everything that you've promised and everything that is in your power, you will have me to reckon with. She's one of your chances; this job of wood-chopping is another; if you don't take as industriously to this as you do to the other, don't ever speak to me again anywhere, in any circumstances, and be careful to keep out of my path Good-morning."

III -- "THEY SAY--"

Although Luce had enjoined secrecy upon Charley, and protested against publicity being given by acts and manners any more than by words, she found Charley's society so pleasant that she had not the heart to forbid him to call frequently. She discouraged all attempts at effusive love-making; but she could not help being interested and cheered by the young man's enthusiasm, for the people of Brundy seldom found anything to be enthusiastic about, and as Luce was a great-hearted creature her lover's irrepressible spirits made good the lack of something which she often felt.

But how can any one keep a secret in a town where the people have only other people's affairs to occupy their leisure moments? Within a week everybody was telling everybody else that Charley Wurring had been three times-- some said four-- to the Grews' since the night of the lecture, and that it must mean something; as Luce was the only adult girl in the family, and there were no young men among her brothers, public opinion was not long in determining what the something was. Luce was not the kind of girl of whom girls in general ask leading questions, but it needs not direct statements to establish anything which a lot of gossips desire to believe, so that in less than another week all Brundy, despite Charley's evasions, regarded the couple as fully engaged, and discussed them accordingly at shops, the post-office, and wherever else men and women chanced to meet.

"It seems too bad," said one of the village pastors at a grocer's, where he chanced to meet old Pruffett. "I am not given to romance-- my calling forbids it, through the stern realities which I am obliged to encounter in the experiences of my flock; but that girl has always seemed to me to be worthy of far greater opportunities than our village affords, yet now she seems to have given herself to a young man who shows as few signs of rising as any one whom I know, and who has much, for which he is not responsible, to keep him down. Two young people more utterly unlike in nature I have seldom met."

"Ah, well," replied Pruffett, "let us hope that it is according to the designs of Providence. If like were always to marry like, the world would soon be full of petrified cranks, Dominie."

"I suppose," said the minister cautiously, "that you are right, on general principles, but I confess that the present application distresses me."

"Every one owes something to the community in which he lives," continued Pruffett. "If there is anything in this story which has no authority but common report-- perhaps it accounts for the wonderful change that has come over the entire Wurring family. Charley is working as hard as any farmer in the county, and his father is working with him, and seems to be taking no liquor."

"Charley's mother looks happier than I have seen her for years," admitted the minister; "I noticed it from the pulpit only last Sunday, and it inspired me in both preaching and praying. All of her children were at church, too-- an unusual occurrence."

"Wurring has picked up a good deal of manliness in some way," remarked the grocer. "I've had to refuse him credit very often of late years-- I hated to do it, for he used to be a good customer of mine; still, a man can't conduct a grocery business on bygones if he expects to pay his own bills. The other day, though, when he bought a small bag of flour, I told him he might as well take a barrel, and pay me out of the wood that he and Charley are clearing from that marsh for Champ and his father, but Wurring flushed up and said rather grandly that he couldn't do it, for the wood belonged entirely to Charley. It wasn't so long ago that he used to beg me for small credits, to be paid when Charley got his pay from the school board."

"Luce herself certainly looks happier than she used to," said the minister.

"Then I guess that everybody ought to be happy," said old Pruffett, although he doubted his own words as he thought of Champney Bruff and his dismal secret. He could not help recalling the days, that strung out sadly into months and years, in which he himself had tried to live down his disappointment at losing Luce's mother.

As time went on, however, people began to whisper to one another that matters did not seem to be as they at first had been with Charley and Luce. The woodpiles multiplied rapidly in the Bruff marshland, and Charley himself grew more and more manly in appearance to those who saw him on his way to work in the morning or returning late at night. He went as often to the Grews', but Luce did not look as happy as usual when people chanced to see her. She certainly did not seem to have stopped liking Charley, for those church-goers who spent their time in looking at other people during service said that she had her eyes upon him almost all the while except during prayer time. Veteran gossips, experienced at cross-questioning in ways that would occasionally put the shrewdest and most self-contained natives off their guard, waylaid Luce's little brothers and sisters and asked many questions, but learned nothing; it was evident, therefore, that the young couple did not converse freely in the family circle. What could the matter be?

"Luce," Charley had said one evening, after the girl had several times rallied him on his unusual solemnity, "you do love me, don't you? I don't ask you to say that you care as much for me as I for you, because there's not as much of me to care for, but--"

"Love you? Indeed I do," murmured Luce, "as much as I know how to. You must remember that it is something new to me, while you say you have loved me a long time. I've never been in love before, nor thought much about it, but you know I am very, very fond of you."

"So fond that no one else could take you away from me?"

"You silly boy," said the girl, with a merry laugh. "What a question to ask. Don't you think you had better drop it and the thought of it, until some one else shows some signs of asking me?"

Charley looked as if he were not entirely sure that the question would keep so long, and Luce succeeded in changing the subject; she had read of such forebodings of lovers-- novels were full of them, and she detested most novels.

The next time he called, however, Charley reverted to the subject, and would not be diverted from it; by this time the girl's curiosity was aroused and she insisted upon knowing what the young man meant.

"Only this," was the reply. "There's a better man than I who has been in love with you a long time, and I don't believe he thinks of anything else."

"Then his mind might be better employed," promptly replied the girl. "But who is he?"

"His name is Champney Bruff," said Charley, looking keenly into Luce's eyes as he spoke. To his infinite relief, yet somewhat to his pain also, Luce burst into hearty laughter as she exclaimed:

"How ridiculous!"

"But it isn't ridiculous, my dear," replied Charley very gravely. "It's serious-- very serious."

"Why, Charley," said Luce, after another laugh-- a long, melodious laugh, with a little wonder in it-- "Champ Bruff never spoke to me more than twenty words in any one day in all his life. Whenever he was near me I felt uncomfortable, for he always looked-- why, really he looked as if he was afraid I would bite him, which I solemnly assure you I never once thought of doing."

"What strange creatures you girls are," said Charley, rather pettishly. "There are some of you at whom a man can't look more than half a minute before they suspect him of being in love with them, while others can't see anything but-- but what isn't."

"But what reason have you to be angry about it, you silly boy?" asked Luce. "One would think, to hear you talk, that you would like me to be grateful to Champ Bruff, and fall in love with him in return. If you really insist upon it, I suppose I could--"

"Stop! Stop, please-- at once'" exclaimed Charley hastily. "Still, I'm awfully sorry for Champ."

"Why should you be?" the girl asked merrily; she scarcely knew what she said or why she said it, for the disclosure had amazed her greatly, and she was not accustomed to being amazed. "Hasn't some poet-- a man poet, too, written, "Tis better to have loved and lost than never to have loved at all'?"

"Has he? I didn't know it, and I don't exactly understand why he did it, but perhaps he had more experience than I in such matters. Don't make fun of Champ, though, please, because his disappointment has hurt him dreadfully."

"Disappointment? Why, he never said a word to me about anything of the kind, and if he had I--" Luce did not conclude the sentence, for she could not. Like all other women of the nobler order, she had not spent much time in dreaming about lovers and longing for them; she had supposed that some day, in the natural order of affairs, some man would propose to her, and she might love him and afterward marry him, but the idea of being loved by a man who, as she had said, had scarcely spoken to her except in the briefest manner, and with whom she had no interests in common-- why, it seemed almost shocking. How could the man have come by so silly a fancy?

"How did you come to know all this?" she asked Charley. "You've been hearing some gossip at the shops or the post-office, I'll warrant-- something said for the sole purpose of teasing you. Quite a lot of people are curious about us, and I'm rather uncomfortable about it. Who told you this ridiculous story?"

"Champ himself," replied Charley.

"What? Are you dreaming?"

"I never was wider awake in my life, dear girl; the thought of it frequently keeps me awake when I should be asleep."

"But you must have misunderstood him," insisted Luce, with the positive manner of an entirely honest and simple nature. "It is he who has given you the chance of work which you are improving so splendidly, according to every one. The best things I hear about you are always accompanied by the expression 'Champ says.' Any one would suppose that, if you were right, Champ must be crazy, for he seems to be doing just what a sane man wouldn't do if he were in love with the same woman as the man whom he is praising and helping. I've heard many strange things and read some others, but really, this is the most incomprehensible, nonsensical thing I ever heard of in my life."

"Do stop laughing!" exclaimed Charley. "Your laughter is the sweetest music in the world, but there's a time for everything, and no good man's troubles should be laughed at by a good woman."

"You're a noble-hearted fellow," exclaimed Luce, with the first look of hearty admiration which the young man had ever seen in her face. It pleased him greatly, but did not prevent what he wanted to say; so when Luce begged him to tell her what he knew, and how he learned it, and insisted upon hearing all the particulars, he told her everything which had happened between Champ and him. When he had finished Luce was silent a long time; finally she said:

"What a noble-hearted fellow he must be! Who would imagine, to look at that serious, matter-of-fact face of his, that there was a single spark of romance in him?"

"Romance?" echoed Charley. "The romance isn't near so wonderful to me as his heroism. If you'd seen him standing there in the woods, his axe upraised, and his face looking as if he wanted to kill me-- you wouldn't have thought there was anything romantic about him."

"And he is doing all this for me," said Luce, who had gone into a reverie.

"He certainly is," was the reply. "He certainly doesn't do it for me. He never speaks to me unless I compel him; he passes me in the street with the merest nod, and with a look as if he were charging me with the basest form of theft. In fact, he has succeeded in making me feel the same way a great deal of the time."

"I'm sure I don't see why," said Luce, roused by her sense of justice. "You can not have robbed him of what he never had, nor of what he had any good reason to believe he ever would have. The idea of my marrying Champney Bruff!"

"It really doesn't seem possible to you?" asked Charley eagerly and with an intent expression of face.

"Utterly impossible," the girl replied. "Don't you too go crazy. What a strange world this is!"

"But you will try to be polite to him hereafter, when you chance to meet him?"

"I shall not only try; I shall be so, for all that he has done for you, and also for what you say he has suffered. I wish, though, that I hadn't heard of it."

"Why so?"

"Because-- oh, because I'm sorry to be the cause of unhappiness to any one, even if the fault is not at all mine. The affair will appear like a nightmare to me; I wish you hadn't told me of it."

"Then so do I; it seems to be my luck to say and do things at unexpected times."

"Don't blame yourself, you poor boy!" exclaimed Luce; then, for the first time in their acquaintanceship, she kissed him, and the kiss took an immense load from Charley's heart.

After that, however, there was a strange change in the ways of the two young people; Charley never again alluded voluntarily to Champney Bruff, but Luce persisted in asking questions about the unhappy man. Did he seem as solemn as ever? Did he still look and act as if he had been robbed? Did he make any more threats?

The subject finally became unspeakably unpleasant to Charley, for Luce slowly lost the cheerful manner which she had displayed toward him from the beginning of their engagement. She never had acted as sweethearts did in the hundreds of romances Charley had read, but she had made him feel entirely welcome, and this seemed a promise of something better in sweeter days to come. Now, however, she began to greet him inquiringly and anxiously; she said she was in constant fear of trouble between him and Champ, and if there should be anything of the kind she would wish she never had been born. She wished, and said so without a blush, that they were able to marry and go away-- anywhere, to any degree of poverty, if only she might not have to be in the same town with a man who was feeling as Champ was said to feel. Charley had read somewhere of a malady called monomania; he knew the meaning of the word, and he felt sure that it described Luce's condition. He tried to dispose of such wood as he had cut, that he might bravely marry on the proceeds; marriages at Brundy were simple and inexpensive affairs, and a wedding trip was an indulgence of which no happy couples dared to think. But winter was still two or three months away; the natives had ample time in which to haggle and chaffer about the price of their winter supply of fuel, so Charley was obliged to delay.

And all the while he was so sorry for Luce. She, the grandest-natured young woman in the village-- she, who never had been subject to the "nerves" of which even young men were occasionally obliged to hear-- became pale, timorous, and sometimes tearful. Her parents blamed Charley, but the girl declared that he was the dearest fellow in the world, and had never said an unkind word to her; if only she could feel at ease about his future she did not care what might become of her. She no longer tried to keep secret her promise to Charley; she announced, almost defiantly, some sage women thought, that they were engaged to be married, and that he was the best man she ever had known or heard of. The family physician was called in, but he could make nothing of the case; the family's pastor talked with her and prayed with her, but went home afterward in a most bewildered frame of mind. Indeed, no one seemed able to give her any cheer but old Pruffett, who shrewdly timed a call upon her mother at an hour when he knew well the good woman was not at home. He was as kind-hearted and tender as he was shrewd, so, almost before she knew what she was doing, Luce was unburdening her heart to him.

"There will be no trouble between them; drop that thought from your mind," said the old man; "but if both of you are as anxious as you say that Charley and he shall be separated, suppose I send Charley out West for me on a little matter of business? It will put some money into his pocket, and take a great load from your heart. In the meantime I will talk to Champ; I happen to be the only person besides Charley who knows how the poor fellow is feeling, and perhaps I can comfort him a little. No one is fitter to do it, for I've been through a similar experience myself.

"You?" said the girl wonderingly. To her, all love was the exclusive property of young people.

"Yes, I. It was a long time ago, but I shall never forget it. Your mother may perhaps tell you something about it if you ask her."

The very next day all Brundy knew that Charley Wurring had taken the stage for the nearest railway station, and what to make of it no one knew, for Charley had bluntly told inquirers that it was nobody's business where he went or what he went for. When Champ heard this his usual reticence deserted him, and he used language so severe about the young man that the town soon had it that Charley had borrowed a lot of money from Champ, and left town to avoid paying it.

No business man, no matter how great his experience or how perfect his methods, ever finds his time entirely equal to all the demands upon it, so old Pruffett did not reach Champney Bruff until that very volcanic person had heard all that the village could tell him about the departure of Charley Wurring. Pruffett was going to break the news to him in a masterly manner and then force upon Champ some counsel which he did not doubt would have the proper effect.

He found Champ in the marsh forest, and also in a state of wrath. No sooner did the younger man see who it was that was intruding upon the solitude which he had sought for himself than he roared:

"A nice end your advice has brought things to, hasn't it? Luce is miserable, and that young scoundrel gone to no one knows where, while I--"

"Excuse me a moment," interrupted the older man. "Some one knows where Charley is; it is I. Charley isn't a scoundrel either; he's far more a man than I supposed. Still more, Luce isn't miserable; I called there this morning, and found her looking and feeling better than at any time in the last two or three weeks. As to you-- but I interrupted you."

"She's looking and feeling better?" asked Champ. "Are you sure?"

"I've the evidence of my own eyes and ears, and her mother is of my opinion."

"Thank heaven!" exclaimed Champ, smoothing his brow somewhat.

"You were saying something about yourself," persisted old Pruffett.

"Never mind about me, if the girl is feeling better," was the reply. "You know very well, if what you told me a few weeks ago about her mother was true, that I don't care what happens to me if she can be happy."

"You've really learned to feel that way, have you?" The old man accompanied his question with a look so keen, despite the age of his eyes, that Champ winced a bit; but he pulled himself together and looked very manly when he finally said:

"Yes! It's been an awful fight, and one that's by no means over. There isn't an unhappier man on the face of the earth than I; I've thought all manner of dreadful things toward that youngster Charley, but I've been true to the girl in my heart all the while. I shall be ready, all my life long, to do anything in my power that will make her happy in any way."

"Good boy! You'll get your reward for it, as I got mine. You may not believe it-- I didn't for a long while-- indeed, I didn't think such a thing possible; but 'twas none the less comforting when it came. But let's see; you said just now that you'd be willing to do anything to make her happy; well, now's your chance."

"Now! What do you mean?"

"I think it would comfort her greatly if you would call and have a chat with her about Charley."

"Call?" gasped Champ, turning pale. "Why, Mr. Pruffett, I-- really, I never made a call on a young woman in my life!"

"Indeed? That's an awful confession. I don't wonder you are in your present condition of mind. The best way to atone is to begin to make amends as soon as possible. That poor girl has been haunted by the fear that you had some dangerous designs against Charley, and I don't believe that any one but you can disabuse her mind of this very painful impression. Do you intend to allow her to go on suffering?"

"How can I? Do go to her and tell her from me--"

"Second-hand news is poor stuff to send to a woman you profess to regard so highly."

"Then I'll write to her-- at once."

"A person can't say much in a letter, at best; he can say wretchedly little to one who wishes to hear a great deal-- and has an undoubted right to."

Champ looked like a criminal being led to execution, but he finally gasped:

"I'll-- call."

"Promise me," said Pruffett, "that you'll go this very evening."

"I-- I promise."

"Good! Now, don't be a coward, Champ. Girls are not ogres, as a rule; even when they are, they have a fair share of manners when meeting respectable young men who they know have put them under obligations. She knows all that you have done for Charley, and she therefore thinks that you are one of the finest fellows in the world. There are thousands of great men and brilliant ones who would be delighted to call on such a woman, with such a welcome awaiting them. Don't be afraid that you won't know what to say; a girl can make any man talk, unless he chances to have lost the use of his tongue. Don't hurry, either; talk all you can about Charley, and say all the good you can of him; if there are some things about him which you're not entirely sure about, give him the benefit of the doubt; it will please her, and you'll feel the better for it afterward."

Champ promised everything asked of him, but he did it all with the manner of a man talking in a dream. The agonies of his preparations for the call need not be dwelt upon, for they were too serious to be laughed over, although the reader could do nothing else. Suffice it to say, that he received a cordial welcome, for old Pruffett had sent the girl word that Champ was to be expected, and that as the affair was very embarrassing to him womanly pity should see to it that he should not be obliged to feel uncomfortable.

Within five minutes after entering the Grews' door Champ felt quite as much at ease as if he were at home, so he had little trouble in asking after Charley.

"He has gone out West, for a little while, on business for Mr. Pruffett," said Luce.

"I heartily hope there is as much money in it for him as there was for Pruffett himself when he went West," said Champ. "I don't know of any one whom I'd rather see make a fortune in a hurry than Charley. There's splendid stuff in that young man, Miss Grew."

"Do you really think so?" the girl asked, with a look from which she could not keep a sign of curiosity. Champ met it as coolly as if it were a man's glance about a matter of business, and continued:

"Indeed I do. I'm personally proud of it, too, for I have had a little to do with bringing it out."

"Indeed you have," replied Luce heartily. "He has told me of all you have done for him, and I want to thank you, myself, for your manly friendship."

"Oh, don't say that, please!" exclaimed Champ, shading his eyes to keep the girl from seeing some thoughts which he feared might betray themselves.

"Then you are not friends, despite what you say about each other?" asked Luce anxiously. The tone of her voice compelled him to drop his hand and say:

"Miss Grew, I would do more for that young man than for any other man on the face of the earth. Can I make that any stronger?"

"No," murmured Luce, although she looked as if there was something else she would like to know. Champ wondered what it was. He was not accustomed to study women's faces, but he was sure that he knew what was in Luce's mind, so he continued:

"If he doesn't come back as soon as you want him to, I'll beg Mr. Pruffett to hurry him home; I'll offer to go out there in his place, if the old man thinks I can do the work as well as he, I'll--"

"No, no, no!" exclaimed Luce. "I don't want him to come back-- not at present, at least. He is-- he doesn't exactly know how, and it is better for both of us that he should be away for the present-- unless your work is suffering through his absence?"

"My work?" echoed Champ. This was a strange place in which to be reminded of that marshland forest! His work, indeed! What would Luce say if she knew how that work had come about? What a gulf there seemed between him and her, although they were sitting face to face, and not three feet apart! The strangeness of the situation affected Champ so strongly that he lapsed into absent-mindedness, and it took several questions to recall him.

After that the delicate subject was avoided for a little while, and Champ was so rejoiced to find that it really was not hard to talk to an intelligent young woman that he soon felt quite at ease-- nay, proud of himself. Besides, as he told himself, he had earned the right to chat with Luce Grew. Well, the right had been accorded him, most unexpectedly, and he was going to enjoy it to the best of his ability. The evening should be one which he would remember for years, and the recollection of it would help him through many a lonesome hour. He would never forget her face either; it had been in his mind for years, but never as it appeared that evening-- never so handsome, animated, so full of cheer and yet full of soul. What a fool he had been to have delayed his pleasure so long!

Had he been more of a "company man" earlier in life, he might at least have numbered Luce among his friends, and who knows what better might have happened if he had enjoyed the stimulus which her face, her eyes, her manner, her voice, her entire presence, now gave him? He tried to analyze it, but he succeeded only in informing himself that it was solely because she was Luce Grew.

Time flew rapidly, but Champ took no note of it. The old clock in the kitchen struck loudly, but Champ did not hear it. For the time being he was in Elysium; yet really they talked only of village affairs and church matters and the doings of the various farmers. How different common subjects did appear when there was such a person as Luce to talk them over with!

Suddenly one of the children entered and handed Luce a letter.

"How strange!" she exclaimed. Letters delivered by hand were as rare during Brundy evenings as snowflakes in May. Suddenly she turned pale and exclaimed:

"Why, it's from Charley!"

With trembling hands she tore the envelope; Champ frowned and arose to go. Even from a distance, and on this one evening of all evenings, that bane of his existence was still active in making trouble for him.

Luce took from the envelope two inclosures, looked at them, and said:

"Why, one of them is for you!"

"Ah, something about that wood-chopping, I suppose," said Champ, opening his letter. It did not take him long to read it, for Charley wrote a large, round, schoolboy hand. The letter ran thus:

"Dear Champ:-- Marry Luce. She knows how you love her, for I had to tell her all about it. That isn't all; she loves you too she couldn't help it after she knew all. That's why I have gone West. God bless you both. Yours always,

"CHARLEY."

Champ looked up, startled by a slight exclamation from Luce. The girl was leaning against the table, upon which she had dropped her letter. Champ did not mean to read it; but the letter itself was so short and the penmanship so large that he could not help getting its entire contents at a glance.

"Miss Grew," said he quickly, although his voice trembled, "I've accidentally seen your letter. It's only fair, therefore, that you should read mine."

He extended it toward her. She took it slowly took a long, long time, it seemed to Champ, to read it, but finally she looked up, smiled timidly, and said:

"Well?"

"Luce!" exclaimed Champ, taking the girl's hands. What either of them said afterward was entirely their own affair.

"I saw how things were going pretty soon after they began to go wrong between Luce and Charley," said old Pruffett to Champ the next day; "and when the boy admitted to me that he had told her all about your confession to him, I made up my mind that it was all up with him, because well, I knew her mother, and it's grand good stock. Eh? Then why didn't her mother take me? Because the other man was the better man, my boy, just as you are the better man than Charley. I doubted her being able-- doubted Luce, I mean, being able-- to give her heart entirely to a youth like Charley, though there are a lot of good points about him; and I hoped that it might turn out in time, as it has, that both he and she would learn their mistake, and that your chance would come. In the meantime, what I said to you, and you acted upon, was just what you needed to make you search your heart and find out for whom you really loved Luce-- for yourself, or for her. That's something that the best men sometimes fail to find out until it is too late, my boy, and they have a world of unhappiness about it."

"But how did you come to send Charley away at just the right time?"

"How? Because the right time had come. I had been giving my own entire time to watching for it. I wonder if those two young people could possibly imagine how closely their affairs interested an old man who was supposed to do nothing but gossip about town and read the newspapers. Charley made a clean breast to me about his trouble. I went to see the girl's mother-- I've already told you about her-- and found things about as I supposed. Then I talked with the girl herself. The rest of it was easy enough."

"Yes, to a man who had business in the West; but suppose there had been no such help for me?'"

"My dear boy," said the old man, "there's an old Western saying that may do you good to bear in mind: 'Never cross a stream until you reach it.' There was a man here to send Charley to the West, so you can afford to drop that part of the subject."

"But everything worked as well as if it had been managed by Heaven itself," said Champ.

"I don't for a moment doubt that it was," replied the old man, reverently dropping his head for a moment. Such things usually are-- when the parties deserve special attention.

"I don't see, though, how Charley timed those letters to arrive just right," persisted Champ. "He must be a thousand miles away by this time. He didn't know that I would ever call at the Grews' in the course of my life."

Old Pruffett looked embarrassed; then he said:

"I've heard that new-made lovers are very slow of perception. Why, you stupid fellow, Charley wrote those letters and gave them to me before he left; he did it, willingly enough, at my own suggestion. I personally made you promise to call last night; then I stood in the night air for nearly an hour, a few rods from your house, to make sure that you did it, even if I had to drag you out and carry you there. Then I followed you, hung about the Grews' for a while, with my heart In my throat, for fear you'd come away soon-- you seemed so scared at the idea of going, you know. Finally I slipped across the street into the yard-- I'm glad the Grews don't own one of those annoying small dogs that bark at every one who ventures upon the premises-- I slipped into the yard, and peeped through one of the windows. Yes, sir, I did. I know it wasn't exactly mannerly, but business is business, and the whole affair was very serious business to me, I can tell you. I saw you both getting along pretty well together, so I thought it would make matters all the easier afterward to let you go on. Finally the night air began to make me so chilly that I had to hurry matters in self-defence, so I slipped round to the back door and got one of the children to deliver the note, first making him promise not to tell who left it. Then I looked through the window again; I really didn't feel comfortable about doing it, Champ, but it was a matter of business with me. I hope your heart didn't thump as mine did while you two were reading those letters I waited until I saw you take Luce's hand, and then-- don't blush-- then I went home, got down on my knees, and thanked God that I had known Luce's mother."

"And poor Charley!" said Champ, with a sigh.

"Ah, well, 'tis better for him to have lost Luce than not to have been in love with her. I loved her mother, and I know."

THE END

www.ingramcontent.com/pod-product-compliance
Lightning Source LLC
Chambersburg PA
CBHW060347290526
45791CB00004B/1575